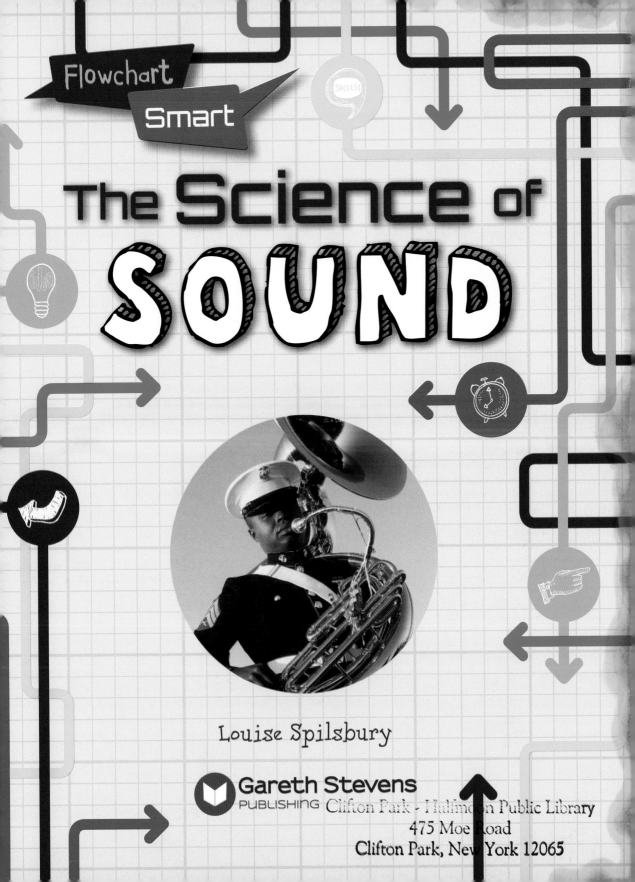

Flowchart

Smart

The Science of
SOUND

Louise Spilsbury

Gareth Stevens
PUBLISHING

Please visit our website, **www.garethstevens.com**.
For a free color catalog of all our high-quality books,
call toll free 1-800-542-2595 or fax 1-877-542-2596.

Cataloging-in-Publication Data

Spilsbury, Louise.
The science of sound / by Louise Spilsbury.
p. cm. — (Flowchart smart)
Includes index.
ISBN 978-1-4824-4150-5 (pbk.)
ISBN 978-1-4824-4151-2 (6-pack)
ISBN 978-1-4824-4152-9 (library binding)
1. Sound — Juvenile literature. I. Spilsbury, Louise. II. Title.
QC225.5 S65 2016
534.078—d23

First Edition

Published in 2016 by
Gareth Stevens Publishing
111 East 14th Street, Suite 349
New York, NY 10003

2229

© 2016 Gareth Stevens Publishing

Produced for Gareth Stevens by Calcium
Editors: Sarah Eason and Harriet McGregor
Designers: Paul Myerscough and Emma DeBanks

Cover art: Shutterstock: Denkcreative, Lineartestpilot.

Picture credits: Dreamstime: Celso Diniz 12–13, Estellerosa 18–19, Gustavo Fernandes
12b, Carlos Soler Martinez 12l, Vadimgozhda 19; Shutterstock: 2studio 2–3, 16–17, AnneMS
10–11, Bacho 11. Bikeriderlondon 26–27, Igor Bulgarin 34–35, ChiccoDodiFC 44–45b,
Everett Collection 20–21, Furtseff 24–25b, KPG Payless 28l, Mphot 29tr, Cristina Muraca 41r,
Ollyy 32–33, Pressmaster 44–45t, Elzbieta Sekowska 40–41, RaJoseph Sohm 1, 28–29, Anna
Tyurina 38bl, Joost van Uffelen 4–5, Paul Vinten 24–25t, Kirsanov Valeriy Vladimirovich 38–39,
Wavebreakmedia 45br.

Printed in the United States of America

CPSIA compliance information: Batch #CW16GS: For further information contact Gareth Stevens, New York, New York at 1-800-542-2595.

Contents

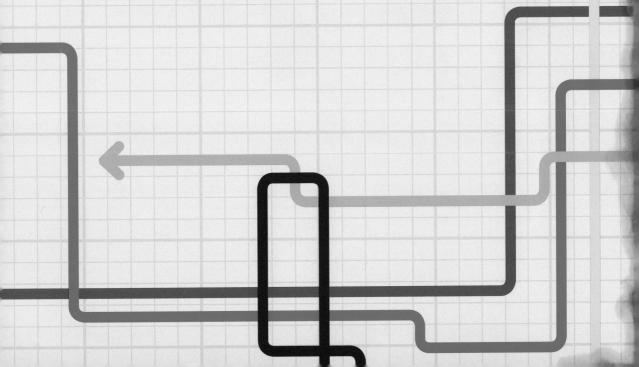

Chapter 1
Sounds All Around

Sounds are all around us. Close your eyes for a moment and listen. What can you hear? Are there noisy cars and buses rushing past in the street and people talking? Or is all you can hear the rustle of the pages of this book and your quiet breathing in and out? Sounds help us communicate, give us information, warn us of danger, and give us pleasure. There are many different sounds in the world, but they are all made in a similar way: by vibrations. When something vibrates, it moves up and down or backward and forward very quickly, again and again. Vibrations are what you see when you pluck a guitar string or tap the skin of a drum, and when things vibrate they make sounds.

When you listen to music, the notes travel toward you on waves of sound.

Sound is never still. It is constantly moving along—in waves! Sound vibrations travel from one place to another in tiny, invisible patterns, which we call sound waves. If you throw a stone in a pond, circles of tiny waves called ripples flow out from the place where the stone fell. Sounds move outward from their source (the thing that made them), in every direction in a similar way. Unlike waves on water, you cannot see sound waves in the air because they are invisible. The sound waves move through the air and we hear them when they reach our ears.

Get Smart!

Some vibrating objects move so quickly that we cannot see them moving. We only know they are vibrating because they make a sound. Some objects make such big vibrations that we can feel as well as hear them—when a big airplane flies low as it comes in to land it can make the windows in buildings near an airport rattle and shake!

Sound Surfing

Sound waves not only move along in waves through the air, but they can also move through water, wood, metal, and other materials. That is how you can hear sounds when your head is underwater in a swimming pool, or from the inside of a room when someone knocks on the door outside. Sound travels better through some materials than through others, and sound moves at different speeds through different substances. For example, sound travels four times faster through water than it does through air.

How exactly do sound waves move? Air and other substances are made up of tiny particles called molecules. When an object vibrates, it makes the molecules around it vibrate, and this creates sound waves. For example, as a bell vibrates back and forth, it pushes against the air molecules that are closest to it. These molecules move forward a little, and push against the molecules next to them. Those molecules also move, and push against the molecules next to them—and so on.

As they shift forward, the molecules leave a space behind them. As they bump into the next molecules, they create a crowded area where the molecules are close together. The bands of empty and crowded air are sound waves.

Whales can communicate over long distances because sound vibrations travel well through water.

Sound cannot travel through a vacuum (an area empty of matter). Between the stars and planets in space you'll find a nearly perfect vacuum. As there is nothing for sound waves to move through, it is spookily silent out in space! On a spacewalk, astronauts speak to each other via radios. They cannot shout across space to each other because there is no air for sounds to travel through.

Get flowchart smart!

How Waves Are Made

Let's look at how sound waves are made once more, using a flowchart.

Molecules make up air.

When objects vibrate, nearby molecules vibrate.

Areas of empty space are created. Areas filled with closely-packed molecules form. Combined, these make sound waves.

SUCCESS

Vibrating molecules push forward into other molecules. These molecules then push into more molecules.

As vibrating molecules move forward, they leave a space behind.

Moving molecules cluster together in a crowded area.

Flowchart

Smart

The outer parts of the human ear, the ear flaps on the sides of your head, are specially designed to collect sounds. These folds of skin are large and form a funnel to collect sounds and channel them along a short tunnel, called the ear canal, into the parts of the ear inside the head.

Sound waves travel along the ear canal until they reach a thin membrane of skin called the eardrum. When the sound waves hit the eardrum they make it vibrate in a similar way to the original source of the vibration. The eardrum passes the vibrations through three tiny bones called ossicles into the inner part of the ear. The ossicles amplify, or increase, the vibrations and pass them into the cochlea.

The cochlea is a snail-shaped tube that contains liquid and 30,000 tiny nerves called hair cells, which look like minuscule hairs. Each hair cell receives and codes different sounds. The vibrations move the hair cells and the hair cells change the vibrations into electrical signals that are sent to the brain through the auditory (hearing) nerve. The brain interprets the signals and tells you what the sounds are. This all happens in an instant!

Our ears help us listen for traffic to keep us safe when we are out and about.

Get Smart!

Have you ever wondered why we have two ears instead of one? Having an ear on each side of the head makes it easier for us to determine where sounds are coming from. The ear closest to a sound hears it slightly earlier and a little louder than the other ear. The brain uses this difference to figure out what direction the sound is coming from.

The cup shape of the outer ear helps it gather sound waves. When we cup a hand around our ear we can hear even better.

Turn It Down!

Your ears allow you to use sound waves to receive valuable information about the world around you. That is why it is important to take care of your sense of hearing and protect your ears.

Loud sounds can damage hearing. The hair cells in the cochlea move back and forth with the vibrations caused by sound waves. Very loud sounds cause strong vibrations that can bend and break hair cells. When a hair cell dies, it can no longer send sound signals to the brain and it can never grow back. That is why workers who use noisy machines wear ear protectors and why you should not have the volume up too high on your earphones when you are listening to music. You can also take care of your ears by not poking anything inside your ear canal, because this can damage the eardrum. To clean your ears, simply wipe gently with a cloth or spray your ears with water from a showerhead.

It is important that people wear noise-canceling headphones if they use noisy machines such as drills.

The gentle sound of rustling leaves is one of the quietest sounds we can hear.

People have hearing problems for different reasons. Deaf people cannot hear any sounds. They can still enjoy music by feeling the vibrations that musicians and instruments make through other parts of their body. Some people with hearing difficulties can hear better by wearing hearing aids. These are devices that pick up sound waves and make them louder and clearer.

The noise made by a rocket taking off is one of the loudest we can hear and can cause immediate damage to hearing.

Get Smart!

The volume of sound is measured in decibels. The softest sound a human can hear is 1 decibel. The sound of breathing is around 10 decibels and an electric drill is 110 decibels. If you are standing close to a sound above 85 decibels, you must protect your ears.

Get flowchart smart!

How Hearing Aids Work

Follow the flowchart to see how a digital behind-the-ear hearing aid works.

A microphone on the outside of the hearing aid picks up sound from the air as it enters the ear. It converts the sound waves into digital signals that are carried into the hearing aid.

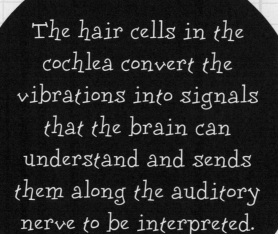

The hair cells in the cochlea convert the vibrations into signals that the brain can understand and sends them along the auditory nerve to be interpreted.

Chapter 3
Loud and Soft

The loudness, or volume, of a sound depends on how much energy is present in the vibrations that create the sound wave. The bigger the vibration, the louder the sound created. When someone knocks hard on a door, they create big, strong vibrations that make a louder sound. They use more energy to hit the door and the sound waves they create contain more energy, too. If someone taps a door gently with their fingers, they create smaller, weaker vibrations that make softer sounds.

If you walk away from something that is making a sound, you will notice that the sound gets quieter the farther you move away from it. This is because sound loses energy as it travels. When a sound wave moves, it pushes the air in front of it. A small amount of energy is used up every time this happens. As energy is used up, the vibrations become smaller and smaller and the sound is quieter and quieter. When the energy runs out, the sound stops altogether. Loud sounds can be heard farther away than softer sounds because they have more energy and can travel farther. Quiet sounds do not have as much energy and they cannot travel as far.

A microchip figures out which sounds need to be improved and passed on, such as the sound of people speaking, and which unwanted background sounds should be reduced.

An amplifier makes the useful digital signals louder and clearer.

A speaker changes the digital signals into vibrations that make weak and distorted signals easier to understand and passes them into the inner ear.

SUCCESS

Get flowchart smart!

How Microphones Work

Follow the flowchart to see how microphones carry sound.

Sound waves enter a microphone and hit a thin membrane. The membrane vibrates.

The electrical signals push and pull a cone in the loudspeaker to make it vibrate. The moving cone makes the sounds louder as it releases the vibrations as sound waves into the air.

SUCCESS

The vibrating membrane causes a coil of wire to vibrate. As the coil of wire moves, it changes the vibrations into electrical signals.

The electrical signals flow through wires to a loudspeaker.

Flowchart Smart

Chapter 4
High and Low

The pitch of a sound describes whether it is high or low. The sounds that you hear around you and when you listen to music come in a range of different pitches. Sounds can be low and rumbling, such as the sounds made by a train or truck, or high and shrill like the squeaks made by a small bird, or anything in between!

The volume of a sound changes depending on the size of the sound waves or vibrations. The pitch of a sound depends on the speed of the vibrations. The number of vibrations per second is called the frequency of a sound. You can think of a sound wave's frequency a little like waves on the ocean. If you see four waves pass a point in one second, you could say the frequency of those waves is four per second. With sound waves, the faster or more frequently something vibrates, the higher the sound. The slower it vibrates, the lower the sound.

A big, heavy bell makes a very low, deep sound.

The longer bars on a xylophone make deeper sounds than the shorter bars.

A tiny bell on a cat's collar makes a high sound.

Percussion instruments such as drums and xylophones are designed to make different high and low sounds when a musician strikes, shakes, or taps them. Bigger instruments make lower sounds. A big drum makes a deeper sound than a small drum, for example. This is because the bigger something is, the longer it takes for the vibrations to move across it when we hit it. A single drum can only play a note of one pitch, but people can use drums to play a tune by lining up a set of drums of different sizes, from the smallest to the biggest. The larger the drum, the lower the pitch!

Changing Strings

Guitars, violins, harps, and double basses are all stringed instruments. They make sounds when their strings vibrate after they are plucked, strummed, or a bow is pulled across them. When the strings vibrate they pass the vibrations on to the body of the instrument, which makes the air inside the hollow part of the instrument vibrate too. This makes the sound waves stronger so that they are louder when they come out of holes at the front of the instrument.

Stringed instruments have different sized strings so that they can play different notes. Heavy, thick strings vibrate more slowly than thin, light strings because the vibrations take longer to travel through them. Musicians use the thicker strings to play lower notes and the thinner strings to play higher notes.

The length of a string also determines its pitch. A double bass is as tall as a man and has long strings. The vibrations have farther to travel through long strings, so they vibrate at a low frequency and create a low pitch. This is why a double bass plays lower notes than a guitar or violin. However, you can change a string's pitch by pressing it and making the vibrating part of it shorter. When the length of a guitar string is changed, it vibrates at a different frequency. Because of this, shorter strings have a higher frequency and a higher pitch.

The long strings on a double bass play low, mellow notes.

Get Smart!

You might be surprised to learn that a piano is a stringed instrument too. Inside a piano there is a set of strings. When you press one of the black or white keys on the outside of the piano, it causes a hammer to hit the strings inside!

Hitting a longer string inside a piano results in a lower pitch, while hitting a shorter string results in a higher pitch.

Tunes with Tubes

Wind instruments include recorders, trumpets, flutes, and other instruments that you blow into to make a sound. Wind instruments are narrow, hollow tubes or pipes with an opening at the bottom and a mouthpiece at the top. They make sounds when you blow into them and cause the air inside them to vibrate. Shorter and smaller wind instruments, such as a piccolo or flute, produce higher pitches. Longer, larger instruments, such as a bassoon or tuba, produce lower notes.

To change the pitch and create different notes, you must make the tube of air inside the wind instrument longer or shorter. On an instrument that has open holes down the front, such as a recorder, you put fingers over the holes to change the length of the column of air. This changes the distance that the air must travel as it vibrates before it can escape through a hole. A shorter column of air creates a higher frequency and a higher note. A longer column of air creates a lower frequency and a lower note. On an instrument such as a trumpet or tuba, you press buttons called keys that cover and uncover holes and change the length of the column of air inside the instrument.

Experiment with blowing through a recorder. The pitch of the note depends on the length of the column of air inside it.

Some wind instruments
have a reed in the mouthpiece.
It vibrates when air is blown into the instrument.

Clarinets and saxophones are a little different because the mouthpiece at the top contains a thin piece of material called a reed. When a musician blows into one of these instruments, they cause the reed to vibrate quickly and this makes the air inside also vibrate. Clarinets and saxophones use a single reed, and oboes and bassoons use a double reed made of two pieces joined together. Flutes are unusual because you hold them horizontally and instead of blowing into the mouthpiece, you blow across it!

The sousaphone makes deep, beautiful sounds. To change the length of the air flow and the pitch of the note you have to press down on valves.

Get flowchart smart!

How a Flute Works

See how a flute makes music by following the flowchart.

A musician holds the flute horizontally with both hands.

He or she blows a stream of air across the hole in the mouthpiece, just as you might blow across the top of a bottle to cause it to make sounds.

The musician covers and uncovers the holes on the flute with his or her fingers to open and close the keys. This changes the length of the column of air, which changes the pitch of the sound.

When the stream of air hits the edge of the other side of the mouthpiece, it is split. This creates a stream of moving air that vibrates the column of air inside the tube.

The vibrating air makes a sound.

Flowchart

Smart

SUCCESS

Chapter 5
Sing and Shout!

Wind instruments convert the energy of moving air into sound energy. The human voice works in the same way! If you close your mouth and make a humming sound while resting your fingers on your throat, you can feel the vibrations that cause the sound of your own voice.

The air we use to make sounds is taken into our body when we breathe. When you breathe in, you take air into your lungs through a tube in your chest and neck called the windpipe, or trachea. When you breathe out, air exits your lungs through the same tube. To speak or sing, you force air up from your lungs and through a part called the voice box, or larynx, at the top of the trachea. Two bands of tissue called vocal cords are stretched across the larynx. These open and close gently all the time when you breathe or swallow. When you use your voice, the flow of air that comes up from your lungs makes these vocal cords vibrate much more quickly and strongly. When the vocal cords vibrate they create sound waves that leave your mouth as sounds.

The energy in the flow of air in your windpipe provides the energy for the vocal cords in the larynx to produce sound. The stronger the flow of air through the vocal cords, the stronger the sound. When you are breathing gently in and out the vocal cords are relaxed and open and do not move very much, so they produce a very quiet sound. When you shout, you use more energy to force air up past the larynx, which gives the vibrations more energy so that they create louder sounds.

> When you speak or sing, the air is forced through the vocal cords and makes them vibrate very fast, from 100 to 1,000 times per second!

Changing Sounds

Musicians open and close holes along the length of a wind instrument to change the length of the column of vibrating air and the pitch of the sounds. Something similar happens to change the tone of the human voice.

When you speak or sing, you change the shape of your vocal cords to change the frequency at which they vibrate. Muscles in the larynx tighten or loosen the vocal cords to change their length and tension. This changes the pitch of your voice. When the vocal cords are tightened they become smaller or shorter. The shorter your vocal cords are and the faster they vibrate, the higher the sound you produce. When your vocal cords are loosened they become longer. It takes longer for the vibrations to pass back and forth across their length, so they produce a lower, deeper sound.

Men and older boys usually have deeper voices than women. This is because their vocal cords are usually longer than female vocal cords, and therefore vibrate at a lower frequency.

Get Smart!

You create different sounds and words by moving your tongue, mouth, and lips. This changes the way that air leaves your mouth and creates different sound waves. For example, to make a "B" sound, you press both lips together and with the vocal cords vibrating, you open your lips suddenly. To make an "F" sound you press your upper front teeth against your bottom lip and force air through the opening before releasing your teeth from your lip. To make an "L" sound you put the tip of your tongue against the ridge behind the top front teeth, vibrate the vocal cords, and quickly release your tongue. Try making different sounds to see how it works!

A choir can create many layers of sound because of the different high and low voices of the male and female singers within it.

Get flowchart smart!

How the Human Voice Works

Find out how the human voice makes sounds by following this flowchart.

SUCCESS

Air comes out of the lungs, up through the windpipe, and into the larynx.

The sound wave is shaped as it travels through the throat and mouth so that by the time it leaves the mouth, it sounds like a voice.

In *the larynx, the* moving air makes *the vocal cords* vibrate.

When *the vocal* cords vibrate, they alternately trap and release air.

When air is released it sends a little puff of air up *the* throat. Each puff of air is the beginning of a sound wave.

Flowchart

Smart

Chapter 6
Using Sounds

Humans and animals use sound in different ways and for different purposes. Some animals make noises by vibrating air in their throat like humans do, although they sound very different because they have different types of voice boxes that vibrate the air differently. Other animals use different body parts to make sound. For example, a cricket communicates by rubbing its legs together to make a chirping sound, and a deathwatch beetle signals to another individual by tapping its head against wood to create a clicking sound.

Animals also have the ability to produce and hear sounds in different frequencies. Humans cannot hear high-frequency sounds over 20,000 vibrations per second, but dogs can. Some dog owners use whistles that their dogs can hear but humans cannot. Some large animals, including elephants, whales, and hippopotamuses, communicate in sound frequencies of below 20 vibrations per second. Sound that is lower than 20 vibrations per second is called infrasound, and humans cannot hear sounds produced by these frequencies. Using infrasound allows animals such as elephants to communicate over long distances.

Dogs can hear much higher pitched sounds than humans.

High-frequency sounds are called ultrasound. Some animals use ultrasound to navigate and hunt. Bats send out pulses of extremely high-frequency sound when they fly at night in the darkness. This is called echolocation. The purpose of echolocation is to help bats avoid obstacles as they fly, and to locate food. When the sound hits an object such as an insect or a tree, an echo bounces back to the bat's ears. Bats listen to the echo to figure out where it came from and how long it took to return. It helps the bat to determine the location and size of an object.

Bats use sound to "see" where they are going!

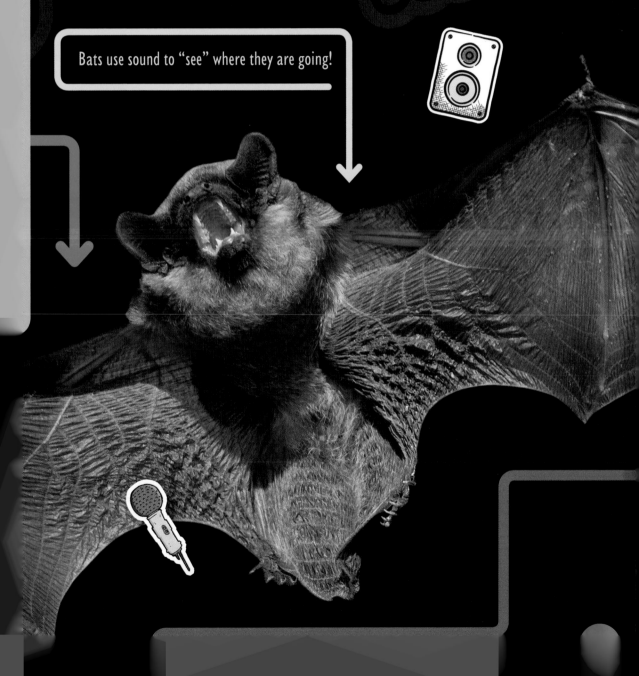

Ultrasound

Humans use ultrasound to help them in different ways. Ultrasound is made by very high-frequency vibrations. You cannot hear ultrasound, but it can be used to scan the deepest, darkest depths of the oceans and even check on a baby while it is still developing inside its mother's body.

Sonar devices use ultrasound to map the bottom of the oceans and to locate objects such as submarines and shipwrecks. Fishing boats use ultrasound to find shoals of fish beneath the surface of the water. Sonar devices transmit high-frequency ultrasound waves from a ship down through the water. When the sound waves hit an object, they reflect back to a receiver in the sonar equipment. The machine measures the number of echoes, the time it takes the echoes to return, and their direction to figure out the size, shape, and distance of different objects.

Boats can use sonar to find fish, shipwrecks, and other objects deep below the ocean's surface.

In hospitals, doctors and nurses use ultrasound machines to look inside the human body and check for diseases, other medical conditions, and to examine an unborn baby. Medical ultrasound machines use sound waves of a very high frequency that produce different echoes when they bounce off different parts inside the body. When an ultrasound device is moved across a mother's abdomen it can send the reflected sound waves into a computer that converts the information it receives into an image of the baby. The image is projected onto a video screen for staff and the baby's parents to see.

Ultrasound waves can be turned into images to show doctors how a baby is developing inside its mother.

Get Smart!

The ultrasound waves used to produce images of unborn babies and organs such as the heart have a high frequency but they are low in energy. This makes it safe for the patients, because high-energy sound waves could damage living cells.

Get flowchart smart!

How Ultrasound Works

Follow the flowchart to understand how ultrasound works.

An ultrasound machine transmits high-frequency sound waves into the human body using a probe.

The sound waves travel into the body and hit the place where two different tissue types meet, such as soft tissue and bone.

The machine displays the information it has gathered from the echoes onto a screen in the form of a two-dimensional (flat) image.

SUCCESS

Some of the sound waves are reflected back to the probe. Others travel on until they reach another boundary and are reflected.

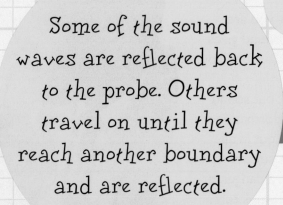

The reflected waves are picked up by the probe and relayed to the machine.

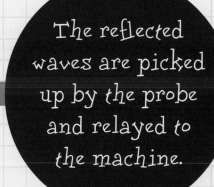

The machine figures out the distance from the probe to the body part by calculating the time it took for each echo to return.

Flowchart

Smart

Sounds and Us

Sound is a vital part of our world. Whether you are walking to school or reading in the library, sound gives you important information about the world around you.

You can see signs that provide information, but sound is an especially important way of sending information quickly and over a distance. Sounds spread out in all directions from their source and can tell us several things all at the same time about an object, a danger, or an event—and even about things that are completely out of sight. For example, when an ambulance or fire engine is traveling fast, it needs to be sure other drivers and pedestrians keep out of the way before it comes speeding down a street. To do this, it uses a siren. You hear the siren long before you see the vehicle. The type of siren can tell you what type of emergency vehicle it is, and you can figure out roughly how far away it is and from which direction it is coming. You may also be able to tell whether it is moving away or coming closer.

Sounds keep us safe! We all get out of the way when a siren warns us an emergency vehicle is coming near.

Sound is vital for communication. You can use it to speak different words and languages and by changing the pitch and volume of your voice you can use sound to express different emotions without actually changing the words! Think about the way you can say "No!" very angrily and definitely, or in a way that suggests someone might be able to change your mind. Those subtle signals are all communicated with just a slight change in the sound of your voice. That is the power of sound!

Sounds help us to learn and communicate, at work, at home, and with our friends.

Sounds give us pleasure, like when we hear live music at a concert.

Glossary

absorb to take in something

acoustics the way that sound travels in a confined space

amplify to make louder or stronger

decibels units for measuring the volume of sound

distorted changed so that is it no longer recognizable as its original form

eardrum the part of the ear that vibrates when sound waves hit it

echo a sound caused by sound waves reflecting off a hard surface

echolocation using echoes to find objects in the dark

energy the ability or power to do work

frequency the number of vibrations per second

interprets perceives. When someone interprets something, they figure out what it means.

loudspeakers machines that change electrical signals into sound waves and release them into the air

lungs the body parts in the chest used for breathing

megaphone a device that is shaped to carry the sound of a person's voice to help it travel farther

membrane a very thin layer of material

microphone a machine that collects sound waves and converts them into electric signals

molecules the smallest identifiable units into which a substance can be divided

nerves the fibers that carry messages around the body

percussion instruments instruments that are beaten to produce a sound. A drum is a percussion instrument.

pitch how high or low a sound is

probe a device that investigates or explores something or an area to gather information about it

reflect to bounce back

sound waves vibrations in the air that we hear as sound

source a person or thing that starts something

trachea another name for the windpipe, a tube in the chest and neck that carries air in and out of the body

transmitted sent

ultrasound a sound of a very high frequency that humans cannot hear

vibrations movements back and forth

vocal cords the membranes across the larynx that vibrate when air goes past them

For More Information

Books

Orr, Tamra B. *Understanding Sound* (Explorer Library: Science Explorer). North Mankato, MN: Cherry Lake Publishing, 2015.

Oxlade, Chris. *Experiments With Sound and Light* (Excellent Science Experiments). New York, NY: PowerKids Press, 2015.

Rooney, Anne. *Audio Engineering and the Science of Sound Waves* (Engineering in Action). New York, NY: Crabtree Publishing, 2014.

Websites

Find out more about how ears work at:
kidshealth.org/kid/htbw/ears.html

Discover more about the science of sound at:
www.explainthatstuff.com/sound.html

At this website you can click on a lot of different animal pictures to hear the different sounds they make:
seaworld.org/en/animal-info/animal-sounds

Index